Read-About® Geography

Living Near the Sea

By Allan Fowler

Consultant
Linda Cornwell, Coordinator of School Quality
and Professional Improvement
Indiana State Teachers Association

SCHOLASTIC INC.
New York Toronto London Auckland Sydney
Mexico City New Delhi Hong Kong Buenos Aires

Designer: Herman Adler Design Group

ISBN 0-516-24178-8

12 11 10 9 8 7 6 5 4 3   4 5 6 7 8/0

Printed in the U.S.A.   61

First Scholastic printing, January 2003

Do you live near the sea?
You may go there to have
fun swimming, playing,
fishing, or sailing.

These girls are building a sandcastle.

People who live near the sea don't always have fun. The sea can flood people's land and ruin their homes.

A house destroyed by the flooding sea.

A sea dam

In some places, people have solved these problems. They have built large dams to keep the sea away from their homes and land.

People who live near the sea often earn their living from the sea.

Some people catch fish for a living.

They ride in fishing boats that set out before sunrise each day.

A fishing boat

The port of Los Angeles, California

Boats set out to sea from a place on land called a port.

Some ports are small villages. Other ports are large cities.

Many people live near ports where cruise ships dock. Cruise ships carry people on vacation trips.

Some of the people sell things to vacationers from the cruise ships, or take them on tours.

Cruise ships in port

These workers are unloading a cargo of bananas.

Ocean freighters carry almost anything from bananas to automobiles.

Many people make their living by loading and unloading goods from the freighters.

In some places, people live near the sea in tall apartment buildings.

These apartment buildings are in Florida.

In other places, people live in small wooden houses.

These houses are on an island in the Pacific Ocean.

Some people don't just live close to the sea. They live right above it.

These homes have been built on wooden poles in the water.

People also live on top
of rocky cliffs that rise
above the sea.

These houses are in
California.

People who live near the sea must pay careful attention to the weather.

Sometimes storms gather over the sea. They move toward land.

The wind and water can destroy buildings.

This storm has caused a flood.

A seawall in Galveston, Texas

Large ocean waves can wash the sand away from a beach.

So people build long seawalls that stretch out from the shore. These walls keep the waves from getting too big.

People who live near the sea like the salty smell of the air. They also like the sound of the waves crashing onto the beach.

Most of the earth is covered by water. There will always be people who live near the sea.

Words You Know

apartment buildings

cliff

cruise ship

dam

flood

freighter

port

seawall

storm

31

Index

About the Author

Allan Fowler is a freelance writer with a background in advertising.
Born in New York, he now lives in Chicago and enjoys traveling.

Photo Credits

©: Liaison Agency Inc.: 5, 31 top left (Lee Celano), 9 (Alissa Crandall), cover (S. Dooley), 10, 31 center (Frank White), 25, 31 bottom right (Gary Williams); PhotoEdit: 28 (Myrleen Ferguson); Viesti Collection, Inc.: 6, 30 bottom right (Walter Bibikov), 22, 30 top right (Richard Cummins), 3 (Michael Javorka), 13, 18, 30 bottom left (Richard & Mary Magruder), 17, 30 top left (Richard Pasley), 14, 21, 26, 31 top right, 31 bottom left (Joe Viesti).

THE BATMAN STRIKES! IN DARKEST KNIGHT

Written by:

Matthew K. Manning

Bill Matheny

Illustrated by:

Terry Beatty

Wes Craig

Christopher Jones

Colored by:

Heroic Age

Lettered by:

Phil Balsman

Pat Brosseau

Jared K. Fletcher

Nick J. Napolitano

Batman created by Bob Kane

Dan DiDio
VP-Executive Editor

Nachie Castro
Editor-original series

Scott Nybakken
Editor-collected edition

Robbin Brosterman
Senior Art Director

Paul Levitz
President & Publisher

Georg Brewer
VP-Design & DC Direct Creative

Richard Bruning
Senior VP-Creative Director

Patrick Caldon
Senior VP-Finance & Operations

Chris Caramalis
VP-Finance

Terri Cunningham
VP-Managing Editor

Stephanie Fierman
Senior VP-Sales & Marketing

Alison Gill
VP-Manufacturing

Rich Johnson
VP-Book Trade Sales

Hank Kanalz
VP-General Manager, WildStorm

Lillian Laserson
Senior VP & General Counsel

Jim Lee
Editorial Director-WildStorm

Paula Lowitt
Senior VP-Business & Legal Affairs

David McKillips
VP-Advertising & Custom Publishing

John Nee
VP-Business Development

Gregory Noveck
Senior VP-Creative Affairs

Cheryl Rubin
Senior VP-Brand Management

Jeff Trojan
VP-Business Development, DC Direct

Bob Wayne
VP-Sales

3-POINTER DISTANCES

A 3-pointer can electrify the crowd and deflate the other team. In the NBA the 3-point line is 23 feet 9 inches from the middle of the hoop to a spot just above the top of the key. The arc is the same distance except for the straight line part, which is 3 feet from the sidelines. Then it measures 22 feet from the middle of the hoop out to the 3-point line.

A 3-pointer is a riskier shot because of the distance, but does that risk pay off? A 3-pointer gets 1.5 times the value of a 2-point shot (3 / 2 = 1.5). You could also say that a 3-pointer is worth 50 percent more points than a 2-pointer.

While the NBA measures 23 feet 9 inches for the 3-point line, college 3-point lines are only 20 feet 9 inches, and most high schools measure 19 feet 9 inches.

When you're at a 45-degree angle to the backboard, it's a perfect time for a bank shot. If the ball hits the backboard at a 45-degree angle, it will leave the backboard at the same angle. Most of the time, if you aim for the square on the backboard from a 45-degree angle, your shot will go right in the hoop.

You can make bank shots from other angles as well, but it's a little more tricky. For example, a 90-degree angle of the ball to the backboard will send the ball right back at you. Usually if a player makes a bank shot from a 90-degree angle, it's by accident.

You can hit a bank shot from anywhere except the sides of the court. From the sides, you are at a 180-degree angle to the backboard, so you don't have room to bank it in.

A circle has 360 degrees, so it has four 90-degree angles.

90°   90°
90°   90°

THERE IS NO "US."

DING

SO, LET'S TALK ABOUT US!

FFFFFFFFT

THEY SNAPPED THE CABLE.

OH POOH. AND I THOUGHT THAT YOU WERE FALLING FOR ME.

CHUD

REAR

KLANK

WE'RE *ALL* SHIVERING IN THIS WEATHER.

ONE OTHER QUESTION COMES TO MIND, MASTER BRUCE: HOW DID FREEZE *ESCAPE* FROM THAT CUSTOMIZED CELL?

SOMEBODY MUST'VE *LET HIM OUT.*

I'M NOT SURE. BUT FREEZE SAID SOMETHING EARLIER TODAY THAT MIGHT--*I HOPE*--PROVIDE ME WITH AN OPENING.

GOOD. I *SHIVER* TO THINK WHAT MIGHT HAPPEN IF HE ISN'T STOPPED.

AND AS SOON AS THIS IS OVER, I'M GOING TO FIND OUT *WHO.*

I WASN'T SURE ABOUT THIS AT FIRST...

...BUT SPRINGING FREEZE FROM THE PEN WAS SHEER GENIUS, *MR. THORNE.*

THAT'S HOW I GOT THE NICKNAME *"BOSS"* THORNE, CLEAR JAY. THE SCHEME IS THE THING!

GOTHAM NIGHTS

FIREFALL

WRITER - BILL MATHENY
PENCILLER - CHRISTOPHER JONES
INKER - TERRY BEATTY
LETTERER - PHIL BALSMAN

46...

47...
48...

...49...
50...

FEEL
THE BURN!
51...

BRRING

HELLO?
YEAH. IT'S
ME...

...FIREFLY.

THESE FLOWERS WILL LOOK WONDERFUL IN YOUR OFFICE, MASTER BRUCE.

THAT'S WHY WE'RE HERE, ALFRED. *ROGER* AND *LIZ* ARE THE BEST IN THE BUSINESS.

ONLY BECAUSE OF *YOU.* KEEPING US EMPLOYED FOR TWENTY YEARS AND *HELPING* US OPEN THE SHOP. YOU'RE QUITE A MAN, MR...

BRUCE.

RIGHT. *BRUCE.*

ALL I DID WAS SPEAK TO THE *OWNER* OF THE BUILDING ABOUT KEEPING YOUR RENT REASONABLE.

YOU OWN THE BUILDING AND *GAVE* US THE SPACE!

SO MUCH FOR BRUCE WAYNE, THE COLDHEARTED, SNOTTY PLAYBOY.

SHHH! IF THIS GETS OUT, MY *IMAGE* WILL BE RUINED!

AHEM. I HEAR THAT A FEW *UNSAVORY* TYPES HAVE STOPPED BY AND THEY WEREN'T SHOPPING FOR BOUQUETS.

ALFRED! HOW DID YOU...

TIME OUT. THIS IS *NEWS* TO ME! IS SOMEONE PUTTING THE SQUEEZE ON YOU FOR PRO-TECTION?

THEY "SUGGESTED" THAT WE COULD B[E] IN DANGER UNLESS WE COOPERATE, B[UT] WE STOOD OUR GROUND.

WE CAN TAKE CARE *OURSELVE[S]* SO DON["T] WORRY AB[OUT] IT, BRUCE.

IS LITA TRAVERS FOR *EXTREME CELEBRITY TRIALS.* E ARE LIVE AT THE GOTHAM CITY COURTHOUSE.

T IS THE FIRST AY OF GOTHAM'S ODDEST COURT HEARING EVER, ATTRACTING THOUSANDS OF REPORTERS AND ONLOOKERS.

I'D LIKE TO WELCOME OUR LEGAL ANALYSTS, JUDGE GRACE HARVEY AND R. MASON BURR.

GOOD MORNING, LITA.

THANK YOU FOR HAVING ME.

HAVE YOU EVER HEARD OF OR PRESIDED OVER THIS KIND OF *SANITY* HEARING, JUDGE HARVEY?

OCCASIONALLY. BUT NO ONE THIS INFAMOUS HAS PETITIONED TO BE TRANSFERRED FROM *ARKHAM ASYLUM* TO JAIL.

AND A MEDIA FRENZY BREAKS OUT AS THE PLAINTIFF ARRIVES, ACCOMPANIED BY AN ARMY OF POLICE OFFICERS.

SECURITY IS THE TOP PRIORITY WITH THIS KIND OF *DEADLY* CRIMINAL, LITA. THAT'S WHY THE COURT CLOSED THE HEARING.

SANITY PLEA

BILL MATHENY - writer
CHRISTOPHER JONES - penciller
TERRY BEATTY - inker
PAT BROSSEAU - letterer

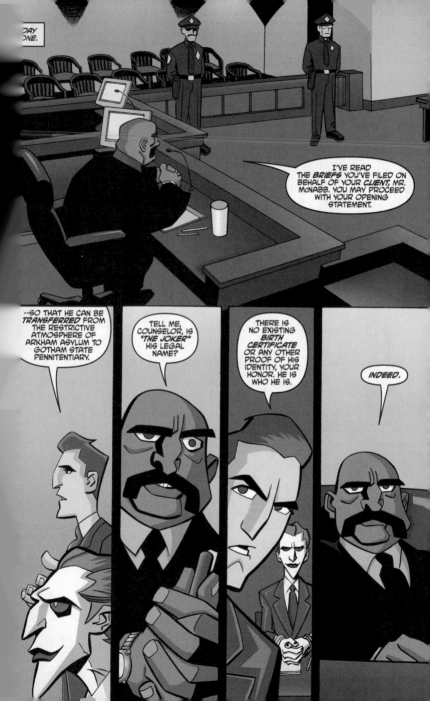

BATMAN?

BATMAN?!?

DAY 14.

WITH THE JOKER INSIDE *TESTIFYIN* ON HIS OWN BEHALF, THE MOC OUTSIDE THE COURTHOUSE IS ELECTRIC.

"NO ONE KNOWS QUITE WHAT TO EXPECT WHEN HE EMERGES FROM THE HEARING."

THIS IS NUMBER TWO. I'M IN PLACE FIFTEEN BLOCKS DUE SOUTH OF THE COURTHOUSE.

NUMBER THREE IN PLACE FIFTEEN BLOCKS DUE WEST OF THE COURTHOUSE.

OUTSTANDING. NOW ADJUST AND PROGRAM YOUR SCOPES.

CLick

ALWAYS ARKHAM.

ILLUMINATION

MATTHEW K. MANNING–writer
TERRY BEATTY–inker
WES CRAIG–penciller
PAT BROSSEAU–letterer

...ISN'T AS MUCH FUN AS THE BROCHURE LED ME TO BELIEVE.

JUST GIMME A SECOND.

HURRY... PLEASE... PLEASE...

CORRECT ME IF I'M WRONG, BUT I COULDA' SWORN THIS PLACE HAD LIGHTS A MINUTE AGO.

HURRY... PLEASE... PLEASE...

THIS GUY GOT KNOCKED OUT COLD, BUT HE OUGHTA HAVE... WAIT. THERE. HERE WE GO...

...THAT'S BETTER.

...OH NO...OH GOD...

ALSO, I SEEM TO RECALL A FEELING OF SECURITY. AND NOW...NOT SO MUCH.

click

THIS COULD QUITE POSSIBLY GO DOWN IN HISTORY AS THE WORST FIELD TRIP OF ALL TIME.

KIRK LANGSTROM. MAN-BAT.

HOW DID YOU GET OUT, KIRK?

HOW DID YOU START ALL THIS?

AIIEEEEEEEEE!!!!

CRUNCH

CRISH

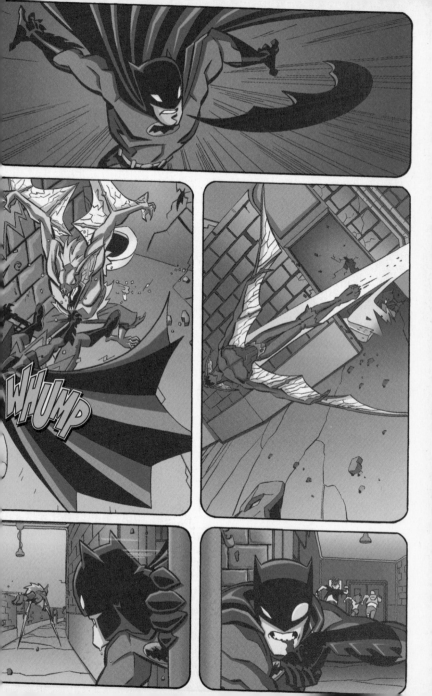

WHUMP

PANT
PANT
PANT

AllEEEEEEEEE!!!!

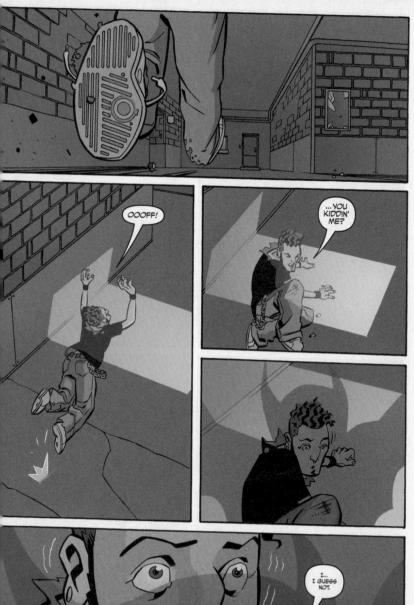

OH GOD.

THAT WAS JESSE. DREW. THAT WAS JESSE. HE GOT HIM, HE GOT...

WAIT, HOLD UP. JUST CALM DOWN A SECOND.

THINK ABOUT IT. YOU KNOW JESS, HE PROBABLY JUST GOT FREAKED OUT AGAIN OR SOMETHING.

YOU STAY HERE AND I'LL HAVE A LOOK. THEN WE CAN GET OUT OF HERE.

JUST STAY PUT, HEIDI.

STAY PUT.

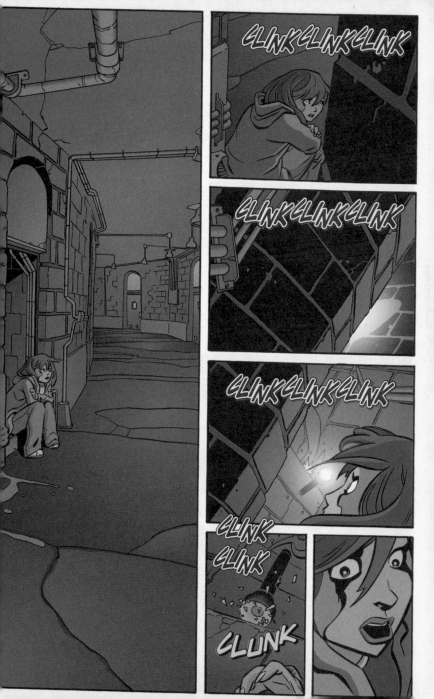

RING RING RING

HELLO?

DR. LANGSTROM... NO, OF COURSE I REMEMBER YOU. COME ON, I MEAN IF YOU WEREN'T THERE TO BAIL ME OUT, I WOULD'VE BEEN EXPELLED BY NOW.

NO, THEY TOOK IT OFF MY RECORD AND EVERYTHING, THANKS TO YOU.

I HEARD, I HEARD. WHAT? UH-HUH. THERE'S A FIELD TRIP THERE LATER THIS WEEK. PSYCHOLOGY CLASS.

OF COURSE I'M GOING.

SURE. YOUR OLD LAB ON WHAT WAS IT, THE THIRD FLOOR? YEAH, REMEMBER.

YEAH, SURE. SURE, I CAN DO THAT.

NO, I UNDERSTAND COMPLETELY. HEY, FOR WHAT YOU DID FOR ME...

"...YOU SCRATCH MY BACK, I SCRATCH YOURS, RIGHT?"

LANGSTROM.

WE'RE NOT FINISHED YET.

SCREEEEEEEEEEE!!!

HE SHOULD BE AROUND HERE SOME...

...THERE!

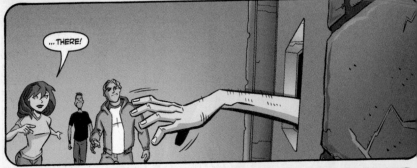

IT WAS RIGHT WHERE YOU TOLD ME IT WOULD BE, DR. LANGSTROM. RIGHT IN THE BACK OF THE CABINET.

GOOD, GOOD. THIS OUGHT TO DO JUST FINE.

WAIT, I THOUGHT YOU SAID... DOCTOR?

"BRING IT OUT INTO THE LIGHT."

END

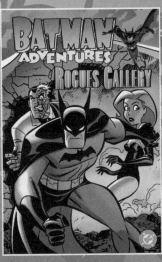